Barrel Racing

Josepha Sherman

Heinemann Library
Chicago, Illinois

Designed by Lisa Buckley
Printed in Hong Kong

04 03 02 01 00
10 9 8 7 6 5 4 3 2 1

Library of Congress Cataloging-in-Publication Data
Sherman, Josepha.
    Barrel racing / Josepha Sherman.
        p. cm. – (Rodeo)
    Includes bibliographical references and index.
    Summary: Introduces the rodeo event of barrel racing, including its origins, rules, training, and stars.
    ISBN 1-57572-503-7 (library binding)
    1. Barrel racing—Juvenile literature. [1. Barrel racing. 2. Rodeos.] I. Title.
GV1834.45.B35 S54 2000
791.8'4—dc21
                                                                                99-048968

Acknowledgments
The author and publishers are grateful to the following for permission to reproduce copyright material:
James L. Amos/National Geographic, p. 4; Ted Streshinsky/Photo 20-20, pp. 5, 19; The Granger Collection, p. 6; Erwin C. "Bud" Nielsen/Images International, pp. 7, 18, 20; Dan Hubbell, pp. 9, 22, 24; Steve Bly, pp. 10, 15; Jack Upton, pp. 11, 27, 28; Spencer Grant/Photo Edit, p. 12; Gordon Gahan/National Geographic, p. 13; Esbin-Anderson/Photo 20-20, p. 14; James L. Amos/National Geographic, p. 16; Northwind Pictures, p. 17; William A. Allard/National Geographic, p. 21; AP/Wide World, p. 23; Dudley Barker, p. 25.

Cover photograph: Dan Hubbell

Special thanks to Dan Sullivan of the Calgary Stampede for his comments in the preparation of this book.

Every effort has been made to contact copyright holders of any material reproduced in this book. Any omissions will be rectified in subsequent printings if notice is given to the publisher.

Some words are shown in bold, **like this.**
You can find out what they mean by looking in the glossary.

Contents

Fast and Furious Fun

An enthusiastic crowd reacts to a barrel race.

The rodeo audience sits forward in anticipation in the **grandstand**. On the arena floor, three barrels have been set out in a carefully measured triangle. The announcer states the name of the first contestant.

Suddenly the crowd roars with excitement. A horse and rider come racing into arena, charging straight at one of the three barrels. What is going to happen now? Are the horse and rider going to crash into the barrel?

Just when it looks as though there's going to be a terrible collision, the horse speeds around the barrel. It twists like a cat, in a turn so tight that it doesn't seem possible. Somehow, the horse doesn't fall. Somehow, the rider stays in the saddle. Somehow, the barrel is still upright.

The horse and rider race on, tightly circling the second barrel and then the third barrel. Now they **gallop** across the finish line at full speed, while behind them, the announcer calls out their final time: 13.75 seconds! That's so fast that this horse and rider have almost certainly won.

This fast-paced event is barrel racing, a sport for horse and rider. It is an event that has become a part of every rodeo.

A barrel racer speeds for the finish line.

How Barrel Racing Began

The Assyrians, who lived in the Near East in the first millennium B.C., were excellent horsemen. This relief shows a lion hunt.

The sport of barrel racing is young when it is compared to other rodeo events that began in the early 1800s, such as **calf roping** or **bronc riding**. However, people have been racing their horses around obstacles for hundreds of years. But in the middle of the 1900s, someone, possibly in the state of Texas, set down the rules for barrel racing.

By the end of the 1950s, barrel racing, with all its excitement and quick action, had become very popular with riders and viewers. It was then included as a regular rodeo event. Today no rodeo is complete without a barrel race.

Barrel racing is not a working ranch activity, such as the rodeo event of **steer** roping. But barrel racing does show off the skill of a horse and a rider working together. And unlike other rodeo events, barrel races may be events at horse shows, too. They may even be separate shows in themselves, like the Drysdales Super Series National Barrel Horse Association (NBHA) barrel race held in Oklahoma. In 1998, this huge event had almost three thousand contestants.

Barrel racing horses make amazingly sharp turns around the barrels.

What Are the Rules?

Barrel racing is the only regular rodeo event to use a special course. Before a race begins, three barrels are placed in a triangle on the arena floor. The barrel at the head of the triangle must be exactly 90 feet (27 meters) from either of the two barrels at the base of the triangle. The two barrels at the base of the triangle must be 70 feet (21 meters) apart.

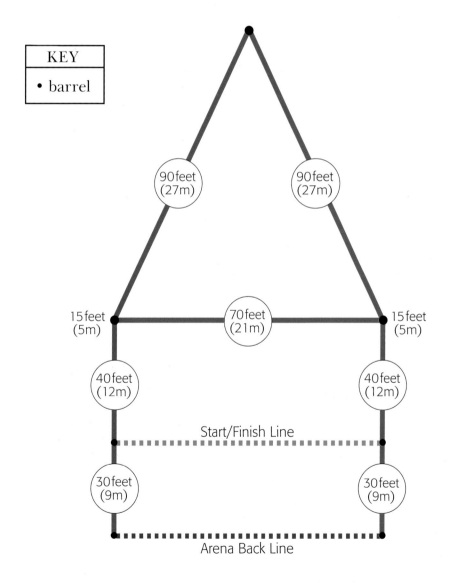

KEY
• barrel

90 feet (27m) 90 feet (27m)

15 feet (5m) 70 feet (21m) 15 feet (5m)

40 feet (12m) 40 feet (12m)

Start/Finish Line

30 feet (9m) 30 feet (9m)

Arena Back Line

To win at barrel racing, a horse and rider must have the fastest time of all the contestants.

Each horse and rider must begin at the starting line. Then they **gallop** onto the course and circle each barrel in turn, running in a **cloverleaf pattern**. They end their race by galloping back across the starting line.

A horse and rider may not miss, knock over, or go the wrong way around a barrel. It's all right to brush a barrel, and it might wobble, but it may not fall over. Knocking a barrel over means a five-second penalty. Missing a barrel means that the horse and rider are disqualified. In professional rodeos where championships are at stake, an automatic **electric eye** measures a horse and rider's time to hundredths of a second.

The Riders

Barrel racing is the only official rodeo sport in which the contestants are usually girls or women. There are no rules that boys or men can't compete. In fact, boys often do compete with girls at smaller rodeos.

There are no rules about how young or old riders must be, either. There have been competitors as young as five years old, while the youngest barrel-racing girl to qualify for the professional rodeo was only twelve. It is not unusual to see teenage girls competing against adult women.

A young barrel racer shows off her skill.

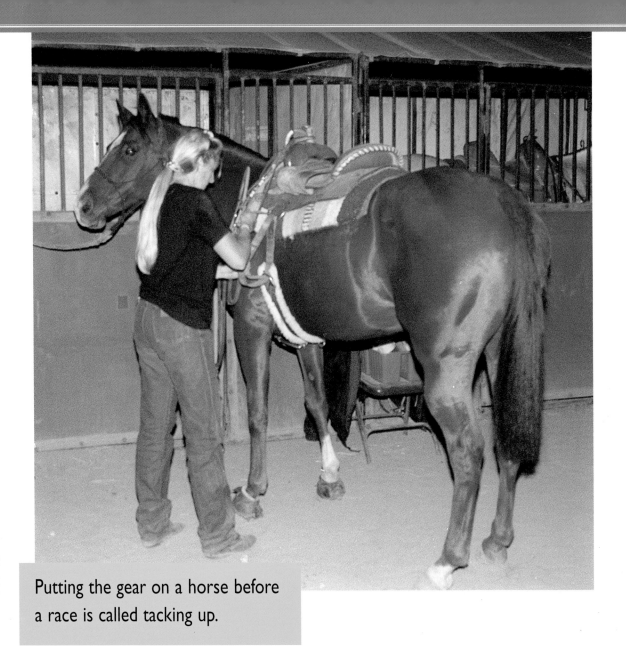

Putting the gear on a horse before
a race is called tacking up.

One of the reasons for the popularity of barrel racing is that
anyone who can ride and has a willing horse can try it. Of
course, the high speeds and quick turns are for professionals,
but even a beginner, reining her horse around a barrel at a
walk or **trot**, can get a feel for the sport.

A professional barrel racer does not have to own her own
horse, though many do. She may ride a horse that belongs
to either another person or to a racing stable.

The Horses

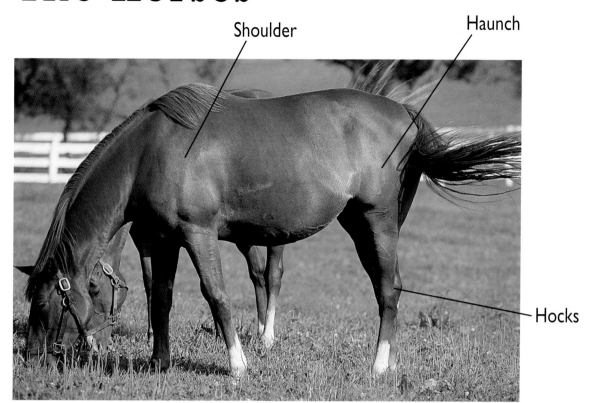

Shoulder

Haunch

Hocks

Good barrel horses come in all colors and sizes. Some are little more than ponies. The horses don't have to be of any special breed. About the only thing barrel horses share in common is their basic shape. This is called conformation. A horse is considered an adult at age four. It is rare to see a horse younger than that in barrel racing. Sometimes a barrel-racing horse in its teens still competes.

Some barrel horses cost thousands of dollars and come from champion barrel horse **sires** and **dams**. Others can be bought for only two or three hundred dollars. Besides conformation, a good barrel horse needs speed, agility to make tight turns around the barrels, and a desire to win.

One breed of horse does show up in barrel races more often than any other. That is the **American quarter horse**. A quarter horse isn't a fourth of anything. The breed got its name because a quarter horse can run a quarter of a mile (402 meters) faster than any other horse. It is also very quick on its feet and is known for intelligence and a calm nature. This combination makes it a good ranch horse and a perfect choice for barrel racing.

Quarter horses leap from the start gate at the beginning of a race.

Training the Rider

Of course, a barrel racer must first know how to ride well. All rodeo riders use the Western style of riding that comes from ranch life. A Western saddle is heavy. It has a raised **pommel**, or **horn**, at the front. A Western horse is neck reined. This means that in order to turn left, a rider places the right rein against the horse's neck. This tells the horse to turn away from that rein and turn left.

Cantle

Pommel, or horn

Girth

Stirrup

This rider helps her horse turn by leaning and reining in that direction.

A barrel rider has to remember to give the right cues to her horse, even during the excitement of the competition. If a horse is told to go right when it is circling a barrel to the left, it is going to be confused. And if the rider is looking straight at the barrel she is trying to circle, she might send a confused horse right into the barrel!

It is also natural for a running horse to slow down to make a tight turn. A barrel-racing rider has to remember that safety can be more important to winning than going full speed ahead.

Training the Horse

A barrel-racing horse has to learn what to do in stages.

Training a barrel racing horse takes time and patience. The horse has to understand what it is being asked to do.

The First Step: The rider walks the horse around the barrels, so that it can see the pattern for itself.

The Second Step: The rider **trots** the horse around the barrels.

The Third Step: The rider takes the horse around the barrels at a **lope,** or canter, which is a faster gait than the trot.

If all of that goes well, the horse is finally ready to take the barrel racing pattern at a full **gallop.**

How long does this step-by-step training take? That depends on the horse. One horse may understand barrel racing right away and learn the whole routine in only one or two months. Another horse might take years to master the event. Still other horses may never like the idea of barrel racing.

No matter how long the training takes, a barrel-racing horse must never be too strongly disciplined. A horse that is too afraid to try its best or gets too angry to work is not going to make a good barrel horse. And, like humans, a horse can get bored. A good trainer remembers that a barrel-racing horse needs some time off work, too!

A beginning barrel racer canters slowly around a barrel.

Gear for Horse and Rider

In barrel racing, the rider and the horse may wear protective gear.

What does the well-dressed barrel racer wear? She usually wears a fancy, colorful Western shirt, jeans, and cowgirl boots. She often tops this off with a traditional Western hat. A barrel rider may also wear protective padding on her knees and elbows on the outside of her clothing. This protects her from being bruised if she hits against the barrels during the race.

The barrel horse often wears protective gear, too. **Bell boots** are a type of rubber boot that guard a rodeo horse's feet. A barrel-racing horse's legs are often protected by bandages as well. Colorful elasticized wrappings act like support stockings for horses.

What goes on a barrel horse's head is important, too. Often a beginning barrel horse will be ridden with a **snaffle bit** in its mouth. A snaffle, which is a plain band of metal, is the simplest and gentlest of bits. If its mouth is hurt, the horse won't want to compete. Once the horse has become used to running the barrels and knows what is expected of it, a rider might switch to the **curb bit**. This is the traditional Western bit. Some barrel racers also use a **tie-down**. This is a strip of leather running from the **bridle** to the saddle that keeps the horse from flinging its head back.

Bridle

Tie-down

Curb bit

Bell boots

19

Going to the Rodeo

Once a horse has learned how to run barrels and a cowgirl knows how to ride the barrel pattern, she will probably be eager to enter her barrel horse in a rodeo. But rodeos are noisy places. Horses are whinnying and **steers** are bawling. The crowd is yelling and laughing. On top of all the noise, there's the voice of the announcer coming over the loud speakers.

It can be a scary place for a horse. Calves are being roped and cowboys are being thrown off bulls. There are clowns in bright colors doing strange things that make the people laugh. But the horse doesn't know what's going on! And it can't be told that it's all just for fun.

Backstage at a rodeo, a horse and rider share a quiet moment between events.

Watching is a good way for horses and riders to learn.

If a horse has never competed before, it's a good idea to first let it simply watch what goes on at a rodeo. In fact, all that noise and excitement can be scary for a first-time rider, too! For a new cowgirl who wants to enter the professional contests, simply watching and getting used to what goes on at a rodeo first is a good idea for her, too.

Barrel-Racing Stars

Charmayne James and Scamper

Together, Charmayne James and her horse, Scamper, earned ten world championships from 1984 until 1993, when Scamper was retired. Scamper was entered as a member of the ProRodeo Hall of Fame in the Timed Horse category. He was even honored with a small model horse that was made in his likeness.

Kristie Peterson and Bozo

The 1994, 1996, 1997, and 1998 world championship team of Kristie Peterson and Bozo proves that barrel horses don't have to be expensive. Kristie Peterson paid less than $500 for Bozo. At the time, Bozo, whose **registered name** is French Flash Hawk, was only two years old. He was half-blind and so nasty-tempered that no one else but Kristie wanted him. Since then, this horse and rider have become a true winning team.

Kristie Peterson and her horse, Bozo, show their winning ways.

Martha Josey and Her Horses

Martha Josey, who is still competing, has been riding and winning at barrel racing for over 30 years. She started her professional career in the late 1960s with her first barrel horse, Cebe Reed. Together they won an amazing 52 barrel races in a row. In 1988, she won a medal with her horse Swen Sir Bug at the 1988 Olympics in Calgary, Canada. Today Martha Josey is teamed up with a new horse named Orange Flash.

Trials and Triumphs

There have been problems behind the scenes in barrel racing. The sport is one of the more popular events at any rodeo. But barrel racers weren't getting treated, honored, or paid as well as competitors in the other events. The team of Charmayne James and Scamper won ten championships together, but rodeo officials chose only the horse, Scamper, for the ProRodeo Hall of Fame.

Were these problems created because barrel racing is mostly a woman's event? The barrel racers thought this might be so. In fact, they even considered suing professional rodeo or staging a **boycott**. A boycott would have meant that none of the barrel racers would have entered rodeos at all.

Charmayne James puts Scamper through his paces.

Because of the efforts of riders like Martha Josey, these young riders will be able to win big money someday.

Instead, the barrel racers, led by such champions as Martha Josey and Charmayne James, took a different track. They **lobbied** the professional rodeo officials for several years. They kept their legal arguments in front of those officials and did not give up. Their hard work finally earned results. In 1996, the Calgary Stampede in Canada made barrel racing an equal major event. Other rodeo committees followed in 1998. Rodeo committees now offer barrel-racing prize money that is equal to other rodeo events.

Pole Bending

There is another related event that curious barrel racers might want to try. Although the sport of pole bending isn't often included in rodeos, it is a very old one. There are descriptions of pole bending even from ancient Greece. Nowadays the sport of pole bending is included in many gymkhanas. Gymkhanas are sports events featuring only horseback activities. There are no rules banning men from the event, but the usual contestants are girls and women.

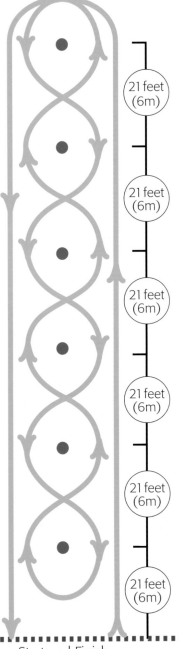

21 feet (6m)

21 feet (6m)

21 feet (6m)

21 feet (6m)

21 feet (6m)

21 feet (6m)

Start and Finish

If a rider in a pole-bending race misses a pole, there is a time penalty.

A successful pole-bending run is every bit as difficult as barrel racing and much more complicated. Six poles are set in the ground at equal spaces in a straight row. The horse and rider begin their run at the starting line at one end and **gallop** along the straight row of poles to the other end. They then ride half circles in and out of the poles, going left, then right, then left, until they reach the last pole. This pole is completely circled. Then the horse and rider go back up the course, tracing half circles in and out again to the top. They finish up with a straight gallop back to the starting line. Touching a pole with a hand or not following the course means disqualification. As with barrel racing, the best race time wins.

Associations

Barrel Racing Industry Council
P.O. Box 9782
Fort Worth, Tex. 76147
(817)737-6397

National Barrel
Horse Association
1355 Reynolds Street
Augusta, Ga. 30901-1050
(706)722-7223
Fax (706)722-9575

Women's Professional
Rodeo Association
1235 Lake Plaza Drive, Suite 134
Colorado Springs, Colo. 80906
(719)576-0900
Fax (719)576-1386

Past Champions

1998	Kristie Peterson	1970	Joyce Burk Loomis
1997	Kristie Peterson	1969	Missy Long
1996	Kristie Peterson	1968	Ann Lewis
1995	Sherry Potter-Cervi	1967	Loretta Manual
1994	Kristie Peterson	1966	Norita Krause Henderson
1993	Charmayne James Rodman	1965	Sammy Thurman Brackenberry
1992	Charmayne James Rodman		
1991	Charmayne James Rodman	1964	Aridth Bruce
1990	Charmayne James Rodman	1963	Loretta Manual
1989	Charmayne James Rodman	1962	Sherry Combs Johnson
1988	Charmayne James Rodman	1961	Jane Mayo
1987	Charmayne James	1960	Jane Mayo
1986	Charmayne James	1959	Jane Mayo
1985	Charmayne James	1958	Billie McBride
1984	Charmayne James	1957	Billie McBride
1983	Marlene Eddleman	1956	Billie McBride
1982	Jan Hansen Smith	1955	Billie McBride
1981	Lynn McKenzie	1954	LaTonne Sewalt
1980	Martha Josey	1953	Wanda Harper Bush
1979	Carol Goostree	1952	Wanda Harper Bush
1978	Lynn McKenzie	1951	Margaret Owens
1977	Jackie Jo Penn	1950	LaTonne Sewalt
1976	Connie Combs Kirby	1949	Amy McGilvray
1975	Jimmie Gibbs Monroe	1948	Margaret Owens
1974	Jeanna Day		
1973	Gail Petska		
1972	Gail Petska		
1971	Donna Patterson		

Glossary

American quarter horse   breed of horse often used in ranch and rodeo work that is known for its speed over short distances, its agility, and its intelligence

bell boot   type of protective rubber boot for horses' feet

boycott   group refusal to enter an event or to buy a product

bridle   straps and metal pieces that fit on a horse's head and in its mouth

bronc riding   timed rodeo event in which a cowboy must stay on the back of a bucking horse for eight seconds

calf roping   timed rodeo event in which a cowboy must lasso a running calf

cloverleaf pattern   four connecting loops that make a shape like a four-leaf clover

curb bit   traditional Western bit that fits inside the horse's mouth

electric eye   device that registers the time at the precise instant a barrel racer crosses its light beam and is accurate to hundredths of a second

dam   mother horse

gallop   fastest gait or movement of a horse

grandstand   seating area in a sports arena

horn   raised front part of a Western saddle, also called a pommel

lobby   present and keep a legal issue before an organization or government

lope   quick movement of a horse that is not the fastest it can go but is faster than a walk; also called a canter

pommel   raised front part of a Western saddle, also called a horn

registered name   official name that a horse is given when it is listed with an association, such as the American quarter horse Association

sire   father horse

snaffle bit   plain band of metal that fits in a horse's mouth

steer   young adult male cattle that cannot reproduce

tie-down   strip of leather running from the bridle to the saddle meant to keep a horse from flinging his head back

trot   movement of a horse that is faster than a walk but not as fast as a canter

More Books to Read

Alter, Judith. *The Greatest Show on Dirt*. New York: Franklin Watts, 1996.

Acton, Avis. *Behind the Chutes at Cheyenne Frontier Days: Your Pocket Guide to Rodeo*. ABC Publishing, 1991.

Kirksmith, Tommie. *Ride Western Style: A Guide for Young Riders*. New York: Howell Books, 1991

Index